My SPANISH Sticker Atlas

Catherine Bruzzone and Louise Millar
Illustrations by Stu McLellan
Spanish language adviser: María Concejo

Índice/Contents

b small publishing
www.bsmall.co.uk

مرحبا 你好

Using this atlas

This atlas will show you how important languages are in our world. The world is huge but we now have the chance to meet and speak to people from many other countries. Of course we can't speak every language in the world but we can be curious and interested and prepared to learn a few words and phrases. Language is the key to making new friends.

This atlas has maps of the following regions:
pages 4-5 North and Central America
pages 6-7 South America
pages 8-9 Europe
pages 10-11 Africa
pages 12-13 Asia
pages 14-15 Oceania (Australia, New Zealand and the Pacific Islands)
pages 16-17 The Arctic and the Antarctic

The countries, mountains, seas and rivers are labelled in Spanish so you can learn lots of new Spanish words. On pages 18 and 19 all the countries are listed region by region according to their number on the maps and with their translation. On page 20 are useful map words with their definite article and translation. On the inside back cover are the answers to questions about the languages of the different regions.

Using the stickers

Each sticker has its name in Spanish. Match the word and picture to the shape and translation on the map pages. You will learn the Spanish names for some important food, animals, plants, industries, natural features, crops and monuments in each region.

नमस्ते สวัสดี

Languages of the world

How many languages do you know? There are thousands of languages in the world and many different alphabets (you can see just a few around the border of this page). The island of Papua New Guinea (see page 14) has over 700! And most people in the world are bilingual, they speak more than one language.

You will find lists of the official or national languages of the countries shown on these maps. The national language is the language used by the government, in education, media and work. Not everyone can speak the national language in their country.

The eight main national languages in the world are: English, Mandarin Chinese, Hindi, Spanish, Russian, French, Arabic and Portuguese. English is used in the most countries but Mandarin Chinese is spoken by the most people.

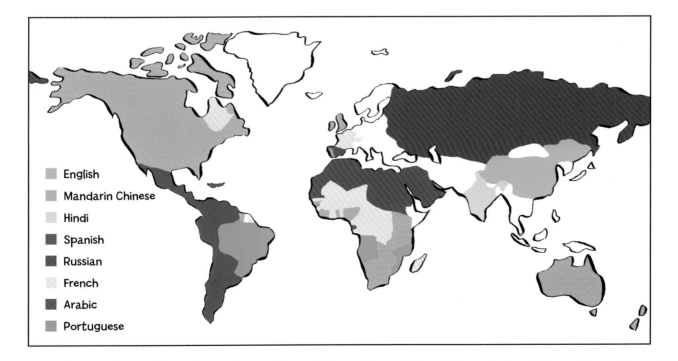

- English
- Mandarin Chinese
- Hindi
- Spanish
- Russian
- French
- Arabic
- Portuguese

OCÉANO
ÁRTICO

río Yukón

Alaska
(EE. UU.)

OCÉANO
PACÍFICO

Hawái
(EE. UU.)

Vancouver ■

Seattle ■

San Francisco ■

Los
Ángeles ■

MONTAÑAS ROCOSAS

BAHÍA
DE HUDSON

1
CANADÁ

2
ESTADOS
UNIDOS DE
AMÉRICA

Gran
Cañón

río Misuri

Grandes
Lagos

catarat
del Niág

■ Chicago

río Colorado

río Misisipí

SIERRA MADRE

río Bravo

GOLFO
DE MÉXICO

■ Ciudad
de México

3
MÉXICO

5 BI

4
GUATEMALA

7
SAN SALVADOR

National languages of North and Central America
There are only three national languages spoken in the countries on this map: English, French and Spanish. Do you know which are the countries where these languages are spoken? Answers on inside back cover.

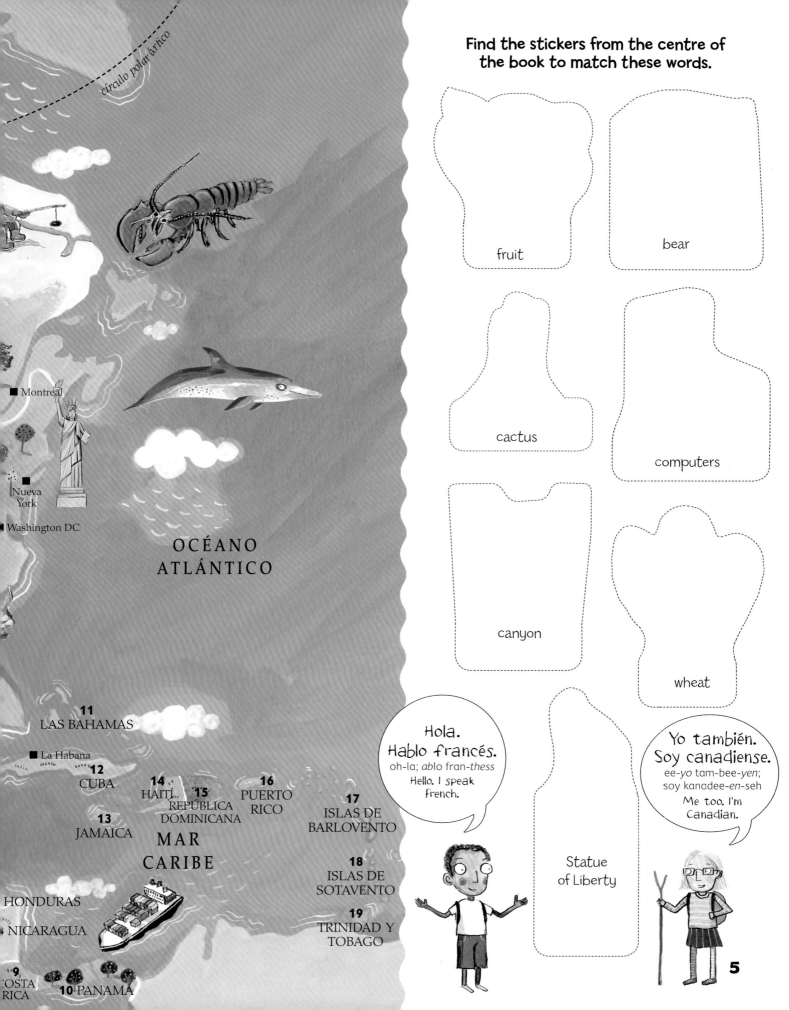

Find the stickers from the centre of the book to match these words.

fruit

bear

cactus

computers

canyon

wheat

Hola.
Hablo francés.
oh-la; *ablo* fran-*thess*
Hello. I speak French.

Yo también.
Soy canadiense.
ee-*yo* tam-bee-*yen*;
soy kanadee-*en*-seh
Me too. I'm Canadian.

Statue of Liberty

5

círculo polar ártico

■ Montreal

■ Nueva York

■ Washington DC

OCÉANO ATLÁNTICO

11 LAS BAHAMAS

■ La Habana

12 CUBA

14 HAITÍ

15 REPÚBLICA DOMINICANA

16 PUERTO RICO

17 ISLAS DE BARLOVENTO

13 JAMAICA

MAR CARIBE

18 ISLAS DE SOTAVENTO

19 TRINIDAD Y TOBAGO

HONDURAS

NICARAGUA

9 COSTA RICA

10 PANAMÁ

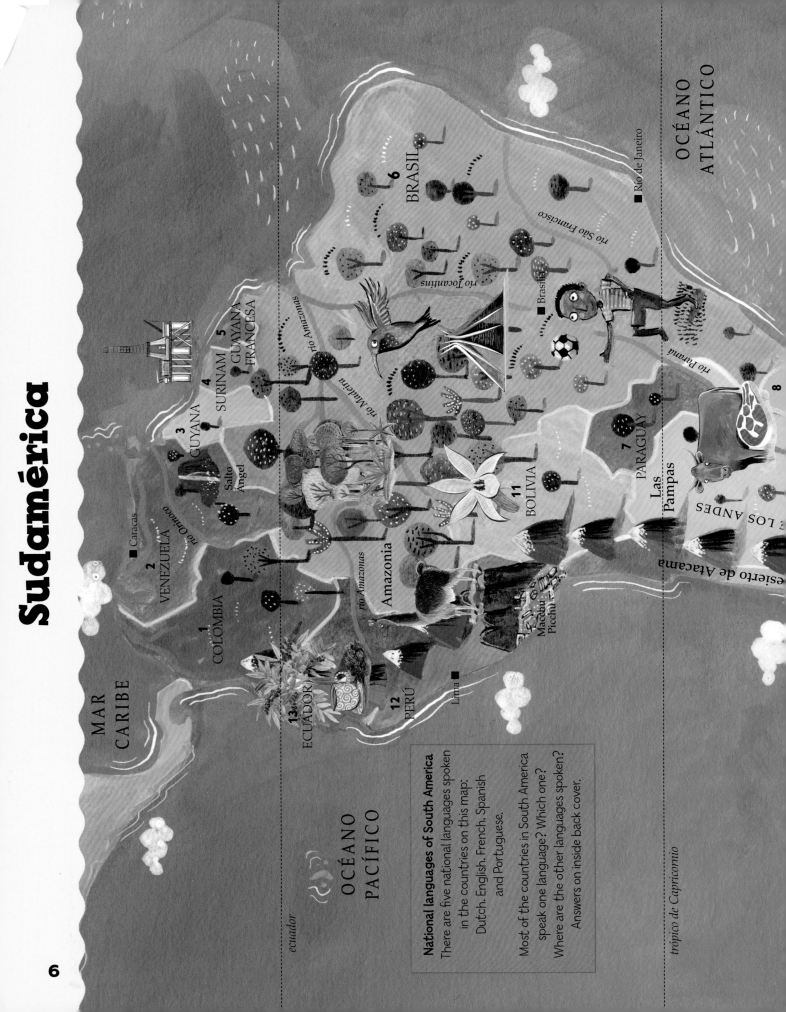

Sudamérica

MAR CARIBE

OCÉANO PACÍFICO

OCÉANO ATLÁNTICO

ecuador

trópico de Capricornio

1 COLOMBIA
2 VENEZUELA
3 GUYANA
4 SURINAM
5 GUYANA FRANCESA
6 BRASIL
7 PARAGUAY
8
11 BOLIVIA
12 PERÚ
13 ECUADOR

Caracas

Salto Ángel

río Orinoco

río Amazonas

río Amazonas

río Madeira

río Tocantins

río São Francisco

Brasília

Río de Janeiro

río Paraná

Amazonia

Machu Picchu

Lima

Las Pampas

LOS ANDES

desierto de Atacama

National languages of South America
There are five national languages spoken in the countries on this map:
Dutch, English, French, Spanish and Portuguese.

Most of the countries in South America speak one language? Which one?
Where are the other languages spoken?
Answers on inside back cover.

6

Find the stickers from the centre of the book to match these words.

llama

cathedral

beef

rainforest

orchid

coffee

oil

No, soy de Brasil. Hablo portugués.
no, soy deh brazeel; ablo portoo-gess
No, I'm from Brazil. I speak Portuguese.

Hola. ¿Hablas español?
oh-la; ablass ess-pan-yol
Hello. Do you speak Spanish?

ARGENTINA

9 ■ Buenos Aires

10
CHILE

CORDILLER

Cabo de Hornos

Europa

1 ISLANDIA

OCÉANO
ÁRTICO

OCÉANO
ATLÁNTICO

2 NORUEGA

3 SUECIA

4 DINAMARCA

MAR
DEL NORTE

EL MAR
BÁLTICO

6 RUSIA

37 REINO UNIDO

36 IRLANDA

Londres
río Támesis

38 PAÍSES BAJOS

39 BÉLGICA

40 LUXEMBURGO

Berlín

28 POLONIA

41 ALEMANIA

río Rin

29 REPÚBLICA CHECA

27 ESLOVAQUIA

30 AUSTRIA

Paris

35 FRANCIA

42 SUIZA

ALPES

26 HUNGRÍA

EL GOLFO
DE VIZCAYA

río Ródano

25 ESLOVENIA

24 CROACIA

río Po

22 BOSNIA Y HERZEGOVINA

23 SERB

PIRINEOS

31 ITALIA

21 MONTENEGRO

20 KOSO

Córcega
(Francia)

Roma

19 MACEDO

Madrid

río Tajo

18 ALBANIA

34 PORTUGAL

33 ESPAÑA

Islas
Baleares
(España)

Cerdeña
(Italia)

MAR
MEDITERRÁNEO

17 GRECIA

Sicilia
(Italia)

32 MALTA

Find the stickers from the centre of the book to match these words.

cheese

sheep

cars

pine tree

river

tomatoes

castle

National languages of Europe

There are 37 national languages spoken in the countries on this map:

Albanian	German	Montenegrin
Belarusian	Greek	Norwegian
Bosnian	Hungarian	Polish
Bulgarian	Icelandic	Portuguese
Croatian	Irish	Romanian
Czech	Italian	Russian
Danish	Latvian	Serbian
Dutch	Lithuanian	Slovak
English	Luxembourgish	Slovenian
Estonian	Macedonian	Spanish
Finnish	Maltese	Swedish
French	Moldovan	Turkish
		Ukrainian

Can you find the countries on the map?
French and German are spoken in several countries. Do you know which?
Answers on inside back cover.

círculo polar ártico

5 FINLANDIA

6 RUSIA

7 ESTONIA

8 LETONIA

9 LITUANIA

10 BIELORRUSIA

río Dniéper

11 UCRANIA

12 MOLDAVIA

río Don

13 RUMANÍA

Danubio

14 BULGARIA

MAR NEGRO

15 TURQUÍA

Atenas

Creta (Grecia)

16 CHIPRE

Buenos días.
¿De dónde eres?
*bway-noss dee-ass;
deh don-deh air-ess*
Good morning.
Where are you from?

Soy griego.
Soy de Grecia.
*soy gree-eh-go;
soy deh greh-thee-a*
I'm Greek.
I'm from Greece.

9

África

MAR MEDITERRÁNEO

MAR ROJO

OCÉANO ÍNDICO

trópico de Cáncer

ecuador

desierto del Sahara

río Nilo

río Níger

río Congo

lago Victoria

■ Cairo
■ Lagos
■ Nairobi

monte Kenia
monte Kilimanjaro

Islas Canarias (España)

1 MARRUECOS
2 TÚNEZ
3 ARGELIA
4 LIBIA
5 EGIPTO
6 SAHARA OCCIDENTAL
7 MAURITANIA
8 SENEGAL
9 GAMBIA
10 GUINEA BISSAU
11 MALI
12 GUINEA
13 BURKINA FASO
14 SIERRA LEONA
15 COSTA DE MARFIL
16 LIBERIA
17 GHANA
18 TOGO
19 BENÍN
20 NIGERIA
21 NÍGER
22 CHAD
23 SUDÁN
24 SUDÁN DEL SUR
25 ERITREA
26 YIBUTI
27 SOMALIA
28 ETIOPÍA
29 REPÚBLICA CENTROAFRICANA
30 CAMERÚN
31 GUINEA ECUATORIAL
32 SANTO TOMÉ Y PRÍNCIPE
33 UGANDA
34 KENIA
35 GABÓN
36 REPÚBLICA DEL CONGO
37 RUANDA
38 BURUNDI
39 REPÚBLICA DEMOCRÁTICA
40 TANZANIA
53 CABO VERDE
55 SEYCHELLES

La comida

lah kom-ee-dah

Food

Norteamérica y Centroamérica páginas 4-5

la fruta

la *froo*-ta

Sudamérica páginas 6-7

la ternera

la tair-*nair*-a

África páginas 10-11

el cacao

el kak-*ah*-o

el chocolate

el choco-*lah*-teh

Europa páginas 8-9

el queso

el *kay*-so

Asia páginas 12-13

el arroz

el ah-*roth*

Australia, Nueva Zelanda y las Islas del Pacífico páginas 14-15

la mantequilla

la manteh-*kee*-ya

Océano Ártico página 17

el ganso

el *gan*-so

Los animales Animals

los anee-mal-ess

África páginas 10-11

el elefante

el ele*fant*-eh

Europa páginas 8-9

las ovejas

las *oveh*-has

Antártida página p 16

el pingüino

el peen-*gweeno*

Norteamérica y Centroamérica páginas 4-5

el oso

el *osso*

Sudamérica páginas 6-7

la llama

la *yah*-ma

Asia páginas 12-13

el tigre

el *tee*-greh

Australia, Nueva Zelanda y las Islas del Pacífico páginas 14-15

el canguro

el kan-*goo*-ro

Océano Ártico página 17

el oso polar

el osso pol-*lar*

Put the gold stars on the countries you have been to, the country you live in now and the country (or countries) your family comes from. Put purple stars on the countries you would like to visit.

Asia páginas 12-13

Norteamérica y
Centroamérica páginas 4-5

Los monumentos

los monoo-*ment*-oss

Monuments

Australia, Nueva Zelanda
y las Islas del Pacifico páginas 14-15

Sudamérica páginas 6-7

la Gran Muralla

la gran m*urah*-ya

el puente de la Bahía de Sidney

el *pwen*-teh deh la *bah*-ya deh *seed*-neh

la catedral

la kateh-*dral*

la Estatua de la Libertad

la ess-*tat*-oo-a deh la leebair-*tad*

Europa páginas 8-9

Antártida página 16

África páginas 10-11

el castillo

el kas*tee*-yo

el laboratorio científico del hielo

el laborat*or*-ee-o thee-en-*tee*-feeko del hee-*eh*-lo

la pirámide

el peer-am-*eedeh*

Las plantas
las *plant*-ass
Plants

África páginas 10-11

la palmera
la pal*mair*-a

Europa páginas 8-9

el pino
el *peeno*

Asia páginas 12-13

el bambú
el bam*boo*

Sudamérica páginas 6-7

la orquídea
la orkee-*deh*-a

Australia, Nueva Zelanda y las Islas del Pacífico páginas 14-15

el cocotero
el koko-*tair*-o

Norteamérica y Centroamérica páginas 4-5

el cactus
el *kak*-toos

Océano Ártico página 17

las algas
las *al*-gas

Las cosechas
las koh-*sech*-ass
Crops

África páginas 10-11

el maíz
el mah-*eez*

Asia páginas 12-13

el té
el *teh*

Australia, Nueva Zelanda y las Islas del Pacífico páginas 14-15

la caña de azúcar
la *kan*-ya deh athoo-*kar*

Antártida página 16

el pez
el *peth*

Sudamérica páginas 6-7

el café
el *kafeh*

Norteamérica y Centroamérica páginas 4-5

el trigo
el *tree*-go

Europa páginas 8-9

los tomates
los *tomah*-tess

Las industrias

las een-*doos*-tree-ass

Industries

África páginas 10-11

el turista

el tour-ee-sta

Europa páginas 8-9

los coches

los *koch*-ess

Asia páginas 12-13

la exploración espacial

la explorathee-*on* esspath-ee-*al*

Norteamérica y Centroamérica páginas 4-5

los ordenadores

los orcenad-*or*-ess

Australia, Nueva Zelanda y las Islas del Pacífico páginas 14-15

las minas de oro

las *meen*ass deh oro

Antártida página 16

la ciencia

la thee-*en*-thee-a

Sudamérica páginas 6-7

el petróleo

el pet-*rol*-ayo

Las características naturales

las karaktair-*ees*-teek-ass natoo-*rah*-less

Natural features

Norteamérica y Centroamérica páginas 4-5

el cañón

el kan-*yon*

Asia páginas 12-13

la montaña

la mon-*tan*-ya

Australia, Nueva Zelanda y las Islas del Pacífico páginas 14-15

el desierto

el deh-see-*air*to

Sudamérica páginas 6-7

la selva tropical

la *selva* tropɜe-*kal*

África páginas 10-11

la jungla

la *hoong*-la

Océano Ártico página 17

el hielo

el *yeh*-lo

Europa páginas 8-9

el río

el *ree*-o

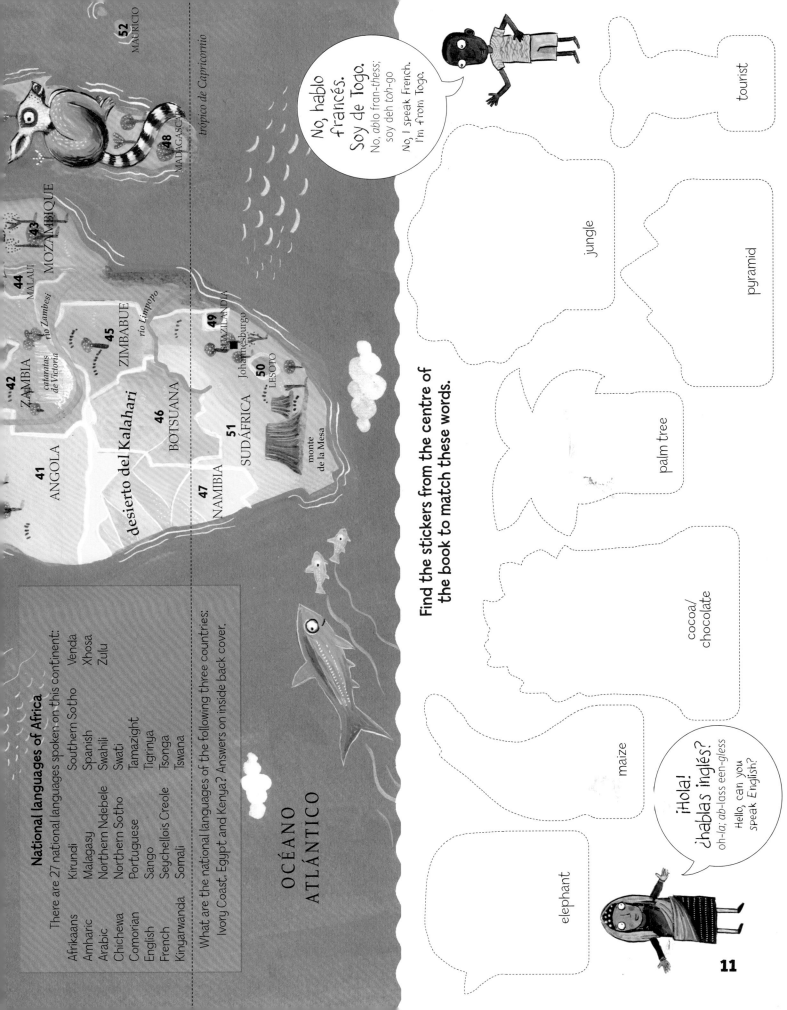

No, hablo francés. Soy de Togo.
No, ablo fran-thess; soy deh toh-go
No, I speak French. I'm from Togo.

National languages of Africa

There are 27 national languages spoken on this continent:

Afrikaans	Kirundi	Southern Sotho	Venda
Amharic	Malagasy	Spanish	Xhosa
Arabic	Northern Ndebele	Swahili	Zulu
Chichewa	Northern Sotho	Swati	
Comorian	Portuguese	Tamazight	
English	Sango	Tigrinya	
French	Seychellois Creole	Tsonga	
Kinyarwanda	Somali	Tswana	

What are the national languages of the following three countries: Ivory Coast, Egypt and Kenya? Answers on inside back cover.

OCÉANO ATLÁNTICO

52 MAURICIO

48 MADAGASCAR

trópico de Capricornio

MOZAMBIQUE

43

44 MALAUI

río Zambesi

ZIMBABUE

45

42 ZAMBIA

cataratas de Victoria

río Limpopo

49 SUAZILANDIA

Johannesburgo

50 LESOTO

41 ANGOLA

desierto del Kalahari

46 BOTSUANA

51 SUDÁFRICA

monte de la Mesa

47 NAMIBIA

Find the stickers from the centre of the book to match these words.

tourist

jungle

pyramid

palm tree

cocoa/chocolate

maize

elephant

¡Hola! ¿hablas inglés?
oh-la; ab-lass een-gless
Hello, can you speak English?

11

Asia

National languages of Asia
There are 38 national languages spoken
in the countries on this map:

Arabic	Filipino (Tagalog)	Lao	Tamil
Armenian	Georgian	Malay	Tetum
Azerbaijani	Hebrew	Maldivian	Thai
Bengali	Hindi	Mongolian	Turkish
Burmese	Indonesian	Nepali	Turkmen
Chinese (Mandarin)	Japanese	Pashtu	Urdu
Dari	Kazakh	Portuguese	Uzbeki
Dzongkha	Khmer	Russian	Vietnamese
English	Korean	Russian	
Farsi (Persian)	Kyrgyz	Sinhala	
		Tajik	

Russian, Arabic, and Farsi (or Persian)
are the national languages in several countries.
Do you know which? Answers on inside back cover.

OCÉANO
ÁRTICO

río Yenisey

río Ob

2
RUSIA

desierto de
Gobi

MAR
NEGRO

1
TURQUÍA

3
GEORGIA

MAR
CASPIO

20
UZBEKISTÁN

21
KAZAJISTÁN

4
ARMENIA

5
AZERBAIYÁN

19
TURKMENISTÁN

22
KIRGUISTÁN

23
TAYIKISTÁN

MAR
MEDITERRÁNEO

6
SIRIA

17
IRAK

■ Teherán

LÍBANO 7

ISRAEL 8

río Éufrates

río Tigris

18
IRÁN

24
AFGANISTÁN

monte
Everest

9 JORDANIA

HIMALAYAS

16
KUWAIT

25
PAKISTÁN

29
NEPAL

■ Nueva Delhi

31
BUTÁN

MAR ROJO

15
BARÉIN

14 QATAR

13
EMIRATOS
ÁRABES UNIDOS

río Indo

río Ganges

30
BANGLADÉS

32
BIRMAN

10
ARABIA
SAUDÍ

27
INDIA

11
YEMEN

12
OMÁN

MAR DE
ARABIA

BAHÍA
DE BENGALA

28
SRI LANKA

26
MALDIVAS

OCÉANO
ÍNDICO

MAR DE BERING

MAR DE OJOTSK

Find the stickers from the centre of the book to match these words.

48 JAPÓN

MAR DEL JAPÓN

■ Tokio

45 MONGOLIA

46 COREA DEL NORTE

■ Pekín

47 COREA DEL SUR

río Amarillo

OCÉANO PACÍFICO

río Yangtsé

trópico de Cáncer

43 CHINA

44 TAIWÁN

■ Hong Kong

33 LAOS

MAR DE CHINA MERIDIONAL

36 TAILANDIA

34 VIETNAM

35 CAMBOYA

42 FILIPINAS

BRUNÉI 41

37 MALASIA

38 SINGAPUR

ecuador

39 INDONESIA

40 TIMOR ORIENTAL

rice

bamboo

tiger

Great Wall

mountain

tea

exploring space

Soy de Japón. Hablo japonés.
soy deh ha*pon*;
ablo hapo-*ness*
I'm from Japan. I speak Japanese.

Soy de Irak. Hablo árabe.
soy deh eerak;
ablo *ah*-rabeh
I'm from Iraq. I speak Arabic.

13

National languages of Australia, New Zealand and the Pacific Islands

There are 14 national languages spoken in the countries on this map:

Bislama	French	Nauruan
English	Hiri Motu	Palauan
Fijian	Kiribati	Samoan
Fijian Hindi	Marshallese	Tok Pisin
	Māori	Tongan

Where do you think English is the national language?
Answers on inside back cover.

Islas Marianas (EE. UU.)

11
ISLAS MARSHALL

9
ESTADOS FEDERADOS DE MICRONESIA

8
PALAOS

10
NAURU

7
PAPÚA-NUEVA GUINEA

■ Puerto Moresby

6
ISLAS SALOMÓN

VANUATU

Nueva Caledonia (Francia)

1
AUSTRALIA

GRAN BARRERA DE CORAL

GRAN CORDILLERA DIVISORIA

trópico de Capricornio

Uluru

río Darling

■ Perth

río Murray   ■ Sidney

■ Canberra

■ Melbourne

MAR DE TASMANIA

2
NUEVA ZELANDA
■ Welli

Tasmania (Australia)

ALPES DEL SUR

OCÉANO ANTÁRTICO

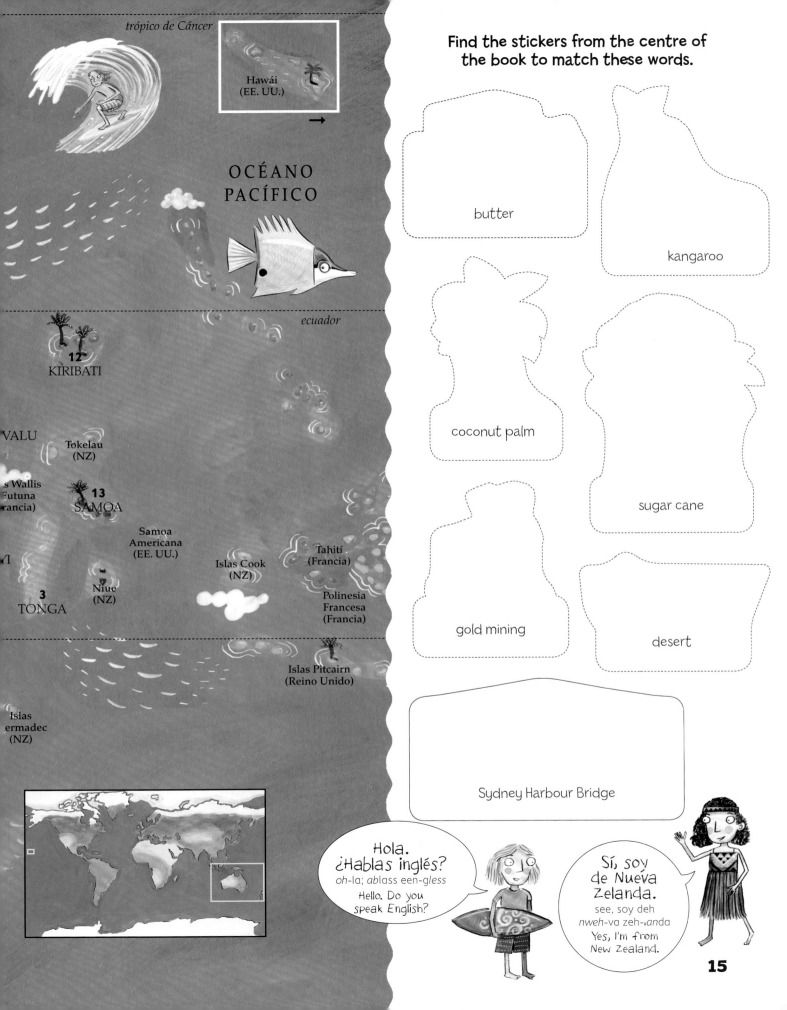

trópico de Cáncer

Hawái
(EE. UU.)

→

OCÉANO
PACÍFICO

ecuador

12
KIRIBATI

VALU

Tokelau
(NZ)

s Wallis
Futuna
rancia)

13
SAMOA

Samoa
Americana
(EE. UU.)

Islas Cook
(NZ)

Tahití
(Francia)

Niue
(NZ)

3
TONGA

Polinesia
Francesa
(Francia)

Islas Pitcairn
(Reino Unido)

Islas
ermadec
(NZ)

Find the stickers from the centre of the book to match these words.

butter

kangaroo

coconut palm

sugar cane

gold mining

desert

Sydney Harbour Bridge

Hola.
¿Hablas inglés?
oh-la; ablass een-gless
Hello. Do you
speak English?

Sí, soy
de Nueva
Zelanda.
*see, soy deh
nweh-va zeh-landa*
Yes, I'm from
New Zealand.

15

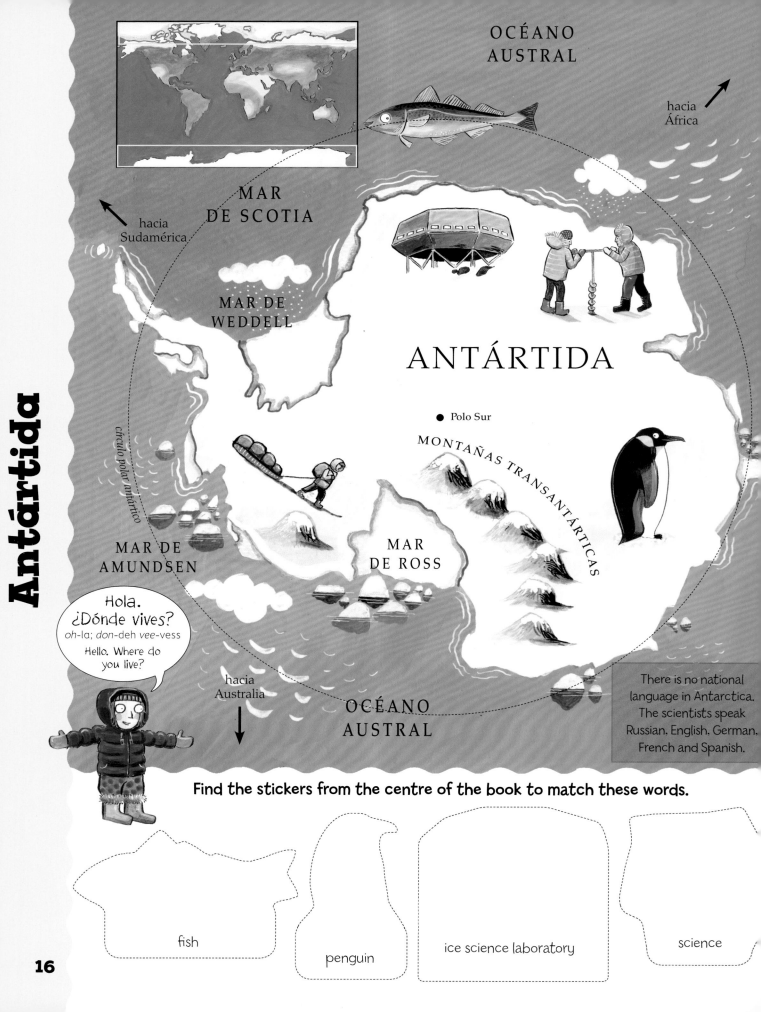

Antártida

OCÉANO AUSTRAL

hacia África

MAR DE SCOTIA

hacia Sudamérica

MAR DE WEDDELL

círculo polar antártico

ANTÁRTIDA

● Polo Sur

MONTAÑAS TRANSANTÁRTICAS

MAR DE AMUNDSEN

MAR DE ROSS

Hola.
¿Dónde vives?
oh-la; *don*-deh *vee*-vess
Hello. Where do
you live?

hacia Australia

OCÉANO AUSTRAL

There is no national
language in Antarctica.
The scientists speak
Russian, English, German,
French and Spanish.

Find the stickers from the centre of the book to match these words.

fish

penguin

ice science laboratory

science

16

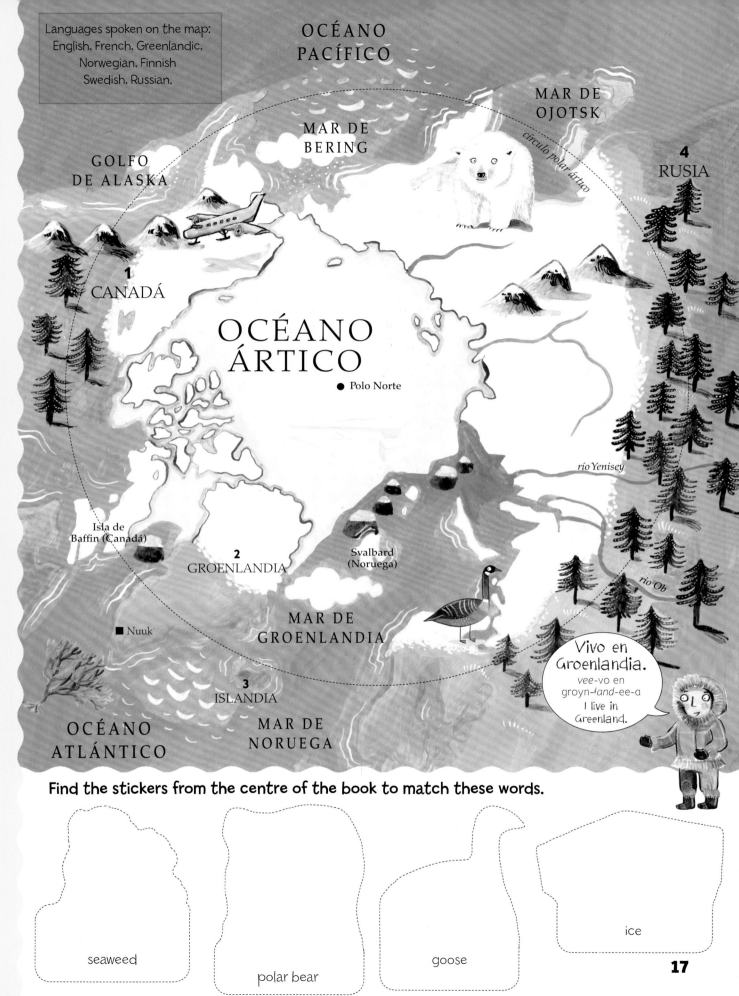

Océano Ártico

Languages spoken on the map:
English, French, Greenlandic,
Norwegian, Finnish
Swedish, Russian.

OCÉANO
PACÍFICO

MAR DE
OJOTSK

círculo polar ártico

MAR DE
BERING

4
RUSIA

GOLFO
DE ALASKA

1
CANADÁ

OCÉANO
ÁRTICO

● Polo Norte

río Yenisey

Isla de
Baffin (Canadá)

Svalbard
(Noruega)

2
GROENLANDIA

río Ob

■ Nuuk

MAR DE
GROENLANDIA

Vivo en
Groenlandia.
vee-vo en
groyn-*land*-ee-a
I live in
Greenland.

3
ISLANDIA

MAR DE
NORUEGA

OCÉANO
ATLÁNTICO

Find the stickers from the centre of the book to match these words.

seaweed

polar bear

goose

ice

17

Los nombres de los países/Names of countries

Norteamérica y Centroamérica p.4
North and Central America p.4

1 **Canadá** Canada
2 **Estados Unidos de América** United States of America
3 **México** Mexico
4 **Guatemala** Guatemala
5 **Belice** Belize
6 **Honduras** Honduras
7 **San Salvador** San Salvador
8 **Nicaragua** Nicaragua
9 **Costa Rica** Costa Rica
10 **Panamá** Panama
11 **las Bahamas** The Bahamas
12 **Cuba** Cuba
13 **Jamaica** Jamaica
14 **Haití** Haiti
15 **República Dominicana** Dominican Republic
16 **Puerto Rico** Puerto Rico
17 **Islas de Barlovento** Leeward Islands
18 **Islas de Sotavento** Windward Islands
19 **Trinidad y Tobago** Trinidad and Tobago
Alaska (EE.UU.) Alaska (USA)
Archipiélago de Hawái (EE.UU.) Hawaii Archipelago (USA)

Sudamérica p.6
South America p.6

1 **Colombia** Colombia
2 **Venezuela** Venezuela
3 **Guyana** Guyana
4 **Surinam** Surinam
5 **Guayana Francesa** French Guiana
6 **Brasil** Brazil
7 **Paraguay** Paraguay
8 **Uruguay** Uruguay
9 **Argentina** Argentina
10 **Chile** Chile
11 **Bolivia** Bolivia
12 **Perú** Peru
13 **Ecuador** Ecuador

Europa p.8 Europe p.8

1 **Islandia** Iceland
2 **Noruega** Norway
3 **Suecia** Sweden
4 **Dinamarca** Denmark
5 **Finlandia** Finland
6 **Rusia** Russia
7 **Estonia** Estonia
8 **Letonia** Latvia
9 **Lituania** Lithuania
10 **Bielorrusia** Belarus
11 **Ucrania** Ukraine
12 **Moldavia** Moldova
13 **Rumanía** Romania
14 **Bulgaria** Bulgaria
15 **Turquía** Turkey
16 **Chipre** Cyprus
17 **Grecia** Greece
18 **Albania** Albania
19 **Macedonia** Macedonia
20 **Kosovo** Kosovo
21 **Montenegro** Montenegro
22 **Bosnia-Herzegovina** Bosnia & Herzegovina
23 **Serbia** Serbia
24 **Croacia** Croatia
25 **Eslovenia** Slovenia
26 **Hungría** Hungary
27 **Eslovaquia** Slovakia
28 **Polonia** Poland
29 **República Checa** Czech Republic
30 **Austria** Austria
31 **Italia** Italy
32 **Malta** Malta
33 **España** Spain
34 **Portugal** Portugal
35 **Francia** France
36 **Irlanda** Ireland
37 **Reino Unido** United Kingdom
38 **Países Bajos** Netherlands
39 **Bélgica** Belgium
40 **Luxemburgo** Luxembourg
41 **Alemania** Germany
42 **Suiza** Switzerland
Islas Baleares (España) Balearic Islands (Spain)
Córcega (Francia) Corsica (France)
Cerdeña (Italia) Sardinia (Italy)
Sicilia (Italia) Sicily (Italy)
Creta (Grecia) Crete (Greece)

África p.10 Africa p.10

1 **Marruecos** Morocco
2 **Túnez** Tunisia
3 **Argelia** Algeria
4 **Libia** Libya
5 **Egipto** Egypt
6 **Sahara Occidental** Western Sahara
7 **Mauritania** Mauritania
8 **Senegal** Senegal
9 **Gambia** Gambia
10 **Guinea Bissau** Guinea Bissau
11 **Mali** Mali
12 **Guinea** Guinea
13 **Burkina Faso** Burkina Faso
14 **Sierra Leona** Sierra Leone
15 **Costa de Marfil** Ivory Coast
16 **Liberia** Liberia
17 **Ghana** Ghana
18 **Togo** Togo
19 **Benín** Benin
20 **Nigeria** Nigeria
21 **Níger** Niger
22 **Chad** Chad
23 **Sudán** Sudan
24 **Sudán del Sur** South Sudan
25 **Eritrea** Eritrea
26 **Yibuti** Djibouti
27 **Somalia** Somalia
28 **Etiopía** Ethiopia
29 **República Centroafricana** Central African Republic
30 **Camerún** Cameroon
31 **Guinea Ecuatorial** Equatorial Guinea
32 **Santo Tomé y Príncipe** São Tomé and Príncipe

Palabras y expresiones de los mapas/Words and expressions on the maps

el río river
el monte mount
la montaña mountain
el desierto desert
el bosque forest
el cañón canyon
las cataratas falls
el lago lake
la isla island
la bahía (de) bay (of)
el golfo (de) gulf (of)
el mar (de) sea (of)
el océano ocean
el cabo (de) cape
hacia... towards...

el círculo polar antártico Antarctic Circle
el círculo polar ártico Arctic Circle
el ecuador Equator
el trópico de Capricornio Tropic of Capricorn
el trópico de Cáncer Tropic of Cancer

el océano Ártico Arctic Ocean
el océano Pacífico Pacific Ocean
el océano Atlántico Atlantic Ocean
el océano Índico Indian Ocean
el océano Austral Southern Ocean

la bahía de Hudson Hudson Bay
el golfo de México Gulf of Mexico
el golfo de Vizcaya Bay of Biscay
la bahía de Bengala Bay of Bengal
el golfo de Alaska Gulf of Alaska

el mar Caribe Caribbean Sea
el mar del Norte North Sea
el mar Báltico Baltic Sea
el mar Mediterráneo Mediterranean Sea
el mar Negro Black Sea
el mar de Ojotsk Sea of Okhotsk
el mar del Japón Sea of Japan
el mar de China Meridional South China Sea
el mar de Arabia Arabian Sea
el mar Rojo Red Sea
el mar Caspio Caspian Sea
el mar de Tasmania Tasman Sea
el mar de Groenlandia Greenland Sea
el mar de Noruega Norwegian Sea

el río Támesis Thames River
el río Tajo Tagus River
el río Ródano Rhône River
el río Rin Rhine River
el río Indo Indus River
el río Amarillo Yellow River
el río Yangtsé Yangtze River

las montañas Rocosas Rocky Mountains
la cordillera de los Andes Andes Mountains
los montes Cárpatos Carpathian Mountains
los Alpes Alps
los Pirineos Pyrenees
el monte de la Mesa Table Mountain
el monte Kenia Mount Kenya
el monte Kilimanjaro Mount Kilimanjaro
los Himalayas Himalayas
el monte Everest Mount Everest
la Gran Cordillera The Great Dividing Range
los Alpes del Sur Southern Alps
las montañas Transantárticas Transantarctic Mountains

el Gran Cañón Grand Canyon
los Grandes Lagos The Great Lakes
las cataratas del Niágara Niagara Falls
las cataratas de Victoria Victoria Falls
la Amazonia Amazon Rainforest
la Gran Barrera de Coral Great Barrier Reef

el desierto de Atacama Atacama Desert
el desierto del Sahara Sahara Desert
el desierto del Kalahari Kalahari Desert
el desierto de Gobi Gobi Desert

el Polo Sur South Pole
el Polo Norte North Pole

Nueva York New York
La Habana Havana
Londres London
París Paris
Berlín Berlin
Roma Rome
Atenas Athens
Teherán Tehran
Pekín Beijing
Puerto Moresby Port Moresby

EE.UU. USA